W9-BCX-932

CPS-MORRILL ELEMENTARY SCHOOL

3488000007424 0

Clemson, Wendy   510 CLE
Using math to be a zoo vet

DATE DUE

510   BC#34880000074240 $18.95
CLE   Clemson, Wendy
             Using math to be a zoo vet
C 1

Morrill Elementary School
Chicago Public Schools
6011 South Rockwell Street
Chicago, IL 60629

MATHWORKS!

Using Math to Be a ZOO VET

by
Wendy and David Clemson
and Ghislaine Sayers

GARETH**STEVENS**
GS
PUBLISHING
A World Almanac Education Group Company

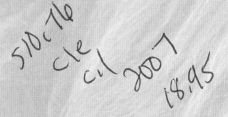

510.76
cle
c.l 2007
18.95

Please visit our web site at: www.garethstevens.com
For a free color catalog describing Gareth Stevens Publishing's
list of high-quality books and multimedia programs, call
1-800-542-2595 (USA) or 1-800-387-3178 (Canada).
Gareth Stevens Publishing's fax: (414) 332-3567.

Library of Congress Cataloging-in-Publication Data

Clemson, Wendy.
    Using math to be a zoo vet / by Wendy Clemson,
David Clemson, and Ghislaine Sayers. — North American ed.
    p. cm. — (Mathworks!)
    ISBN 0-8368-4209-X (lib. bdg.)
    1. Mathematics—Problems, exercises, etc.—Juvenile
literature. 2. Zoo veterinarians—Juvenile literature.
I. Clemson, David. II. Sayers, Ghislaine. III. Title.
IV. Series.
    QA43.C658 2004
    510'.76—dc22   2004047842

This North American edition first published in 2005 by
Gareth Stevens Publishing
A World Almanac Education Group Company
330 West Olive Street, Suite 100
Milwaukee, Wisconsin 53212

This U.S. edition copyright © 2005 by Gareth Stevens Inc.
Original edition copyright © 2004 by ticktock Entertainment
Ltd. First published in Great Britain in 2004 by ticktock Media
Ltd., Unit 2, Orchard Business Centre, North Farm Road,
Tunbridge Wells, Kent, TN2 3XF, England.

The publishers thank the following consultants for their kind
assistance: Jenni Back and Liz Pumfrey (NRICH Project,
Cambridge University) and Debra Voege (Science and Math
Curriculum Resource Teacher).

Gareth Stevens Editor: Dorothy L. Gibbs
Gareth Stevens Art Direction: Tammy West

Photo credits (t=top, b=bottom, c=center, l=left, r=right)
Alamy: 8-9, 10, 12-13, 18-19, 27. Corbis: 2-3, 17, 24-25,
29(tl, tc). Paignton Zoo: 20-21, 22-23, 26. Photodisc: cover,
1, 6-7, 11, 14-15, 17. Ticktock Media: 16-17, 29(br).

Every effort has been made to trace the copyright holders
for the photos used in this book. The publisher apologizes,
in advance, for any unintentional omissions and would be
pleased to insert the appropriate acknowledgements in
any subsequent edition of this publication.

All rights reserved to Gareth Stevens, Inc. No part of
this book may be reproduced, stored in a retrieval system,
or transmitted in any form or by any means, electronic,
mechanical, photocopying, recording, or otherwise, without
the prior written permission of the publisher.

Printed in the United States of America

1 2 3 4 5 6 7 8 9 08 07 06 05 04

CONTENTS

HAVE FUN WITH MATH (How to Use This Book)   4

ZOO VET TO THE RESCUE   6

SEDATING A GIRAFFE   8

TWIZZLE ON THE MOVE   10

A NEW HOME FOR TWIZZLE   12

CHECKING FOR PARASITES   14

WORMING THE PRIMATES   16

AN EMERGENCY IN WOLF WOODS   18

A PLACE FOR THE RED RIVER HOGS   20

AMELIA'S DIET   22

MONEY MATTERS   24

TWIZZLE HAS A BABY!   26

MATH TIPS   28

ANSWERS   30

GLOSSARY/MEASUREMENT CONVERSIONS   32

HAVE FUN WITH MATH

How to Use This Book

Math is important in the daily lives of people everywhere. We use math when we play games, ride bicycles, or go shopping, and everyone uses math at work. Imagine you are a veterinarian at a zoo, and one of the animals you are caring for is seriously ill. You may not realize it, but a zoo vet would use math to treat the animal and help it get well. In this book, you will be able to try lots of exciting math activities as you learn about how zoo vets take care of wild animals. If you can work with numbers, measurements, shapes, charts, and diagrams, then you could BE A ZOO VET.

How does it feel to save an animal's life?

Grab your medical equipment and find out what it is like to be on call at the zoo, day and night!

Math Activities

The zoo vet's clipboards have math activities for you to try. Get your pencil, ruler, and notebook (for figuring out problems and listing answers).

WORMING THE PRIMATES

All of the zoo animals are given worming drugs, called anthelmintics, twice a year because, even if the feces samples collected from an enclosure did not show worm eggs, there might still be an animal in that enclosure that has worms. The samples collected might not have included feces from one or more of the animals. An animal that is known to have tested positive for worms is given worming drugs more frequently. Anthelmintic drug powder is added to a small amount of food and given to the animals when they are hungry. So vets will know how much drug the animals have eaten, the rest of their food is given to them after the food with the drug in it is gone.

Zoo Vet Casebook

A zoo vet figures out the correct amount of worming drugs to give each animal by using the animal's body weight. Each of a zoo's primates needs 25 mg of drugs for every pound of its body weight, so the vet needs to know how much each primate weighs.

The DATA BOX on page 17 shows the weights for many of the zoo's primates. Use the information in the DATA BOX to answer the following questions:

1) Which primate is the heaviest?
2) Which primate is the lightest?
3) Name a primate that is heavier than a male lemur but lighter than a female colobus monkey.
4) One of the primates and its traveling crate weigh 6.5 pounds. (When empty, the crate weighs 5.6 pounds.) Which primate is it?

Animal Care Fact

Sometimes, worming drugs are given to animals in the form of a treat by putting them in foods the animals are not normally allowed to eat. Colobus monkeys, spider monkeys, Diana monkeys, and swamp monkeys get their anthelmintic in mashed banana sandwiches. Gorillas and orangutans get theirs in low-sugar, blackcurrant drinks.

Gorilla Fact

One of the gorilla dens at the zoo has a special platform with scales underneath it. A zookeeper puts some of the gorillas' food on the platform and adjusts the scales to show zero. Then the zookeeper lets a gorilla enter the enclosure. When it sits on the platform to eat the food, the gorilla can be weighed.

A zoo vet examines a ring-tailed lemur.

16

NEED HELP?

• If you are not sure how to do some of the math problems, turn to pages 28 and 29, where you will find lots of tips to help get you started.

• Turn to pages 30 and 31 to check your answers.
(Try all the activities and challenges before you look at the answers.)

• Turn to page 32 for definitions of some words and terms used in this book.

Math Facts and Data

To complete some of the math activities, you will need information from a DATA BOX, which looks like this.

You will find lots of amazing details about wild animals and the work of zoo vets in FACT boxes that look like this.

Math Challenge

Orange boxes, like this one, have extra math questions to challenge you.
Give them a try!

DATA BOX Primate Weight Chart

PRIMATE	ADULT MALE	ADULT FEMALE
gorilla	310 pounds	175 pounds
orangutan	175 pounds	95 pounds
gibbon	15 pounds	15 pounds
ring-tailed lemur	9 pounds	8 pounds
howler monkey	20 pounds	20 pounds
golden lion tamarin	14 ounces	14 ounces
Goeldi monkey	12 ounces	12 ounces
colobus monkey	27 pounds	20 pounds
spider monkey	24 pounds	24 pounds
Diana monkey	21 pounds	21 pounds
swamp monkey	20 pounds	20 pounds

Math Challenge

Try to answer this fun question! On one end of a seesaw are 5 golden lion tamarins and 1 female colobus monkey.

Which primate sitting on the other end of the seesaw would be the closest in weight to make the seesaw balance?

17

5

ZOO VET TO THE RESCUE

You have just received an emergency phone call from another zoo that is hundreds of miles away. The other zoo has been flooded, and their female giraffe, called Twizzle, urgently needs a new home. Your zoo has an enclosure for giraffes, as well as a male giraffe who is waiting for a mate. You quickly agree that Twizzle can come to live at your zoo. First, you need to find a way to transport the giraffe. The zoo's truck is big enough to carry Twizzle, but she will need to be inside a smaller crate for traveling. Because you are the zoo vet, you must arrange to have this crate built as quickly as possible!

Zoo Vet Casebook

The zoo's maintenance workers have drawn some designs for the giraffe's traveling crate. All of the designs use materials strong enough to withstand Twizzle's kicks, but you need to think about all her other needs.

Your specifications for the crate are as follows:

- The crate must be slightly higher than Twizzle.
- Twizzle must be able to sit down, stand up, and turn around in her crate.
- The crate should have a roof made of fine netting or burlap (coarse fabric).
- The crate must have ventilation (air holes), but the ventilation holes must not be so large that Twizzle's horns could get stuck in them or be in a place where she can kick, because the ventilation holes will weaken that part of the crate.

Look at the crate designs in the DATA BOX on page 7.
1) Which crate would you choose? 2) Why?
3) How much space will Twizzle have above her in the crate?

Animal Care Fact

To keep Twizzle clean and dry during her journey, the floor of the traveling crate must allow the giraffe's urine to drain away. The crate has a false floor made from a metal grid so that any liquids can drain through the small gap between the grid and the bottom of the crate. Both the floor grid and the walls of the crate are padded with rubber matting to help protect Twizzle during the journey. The floor grid must be comfortable to lie on, too, so the rubber matting is covered with a thick layer of straw.

body length: 11.5 feet

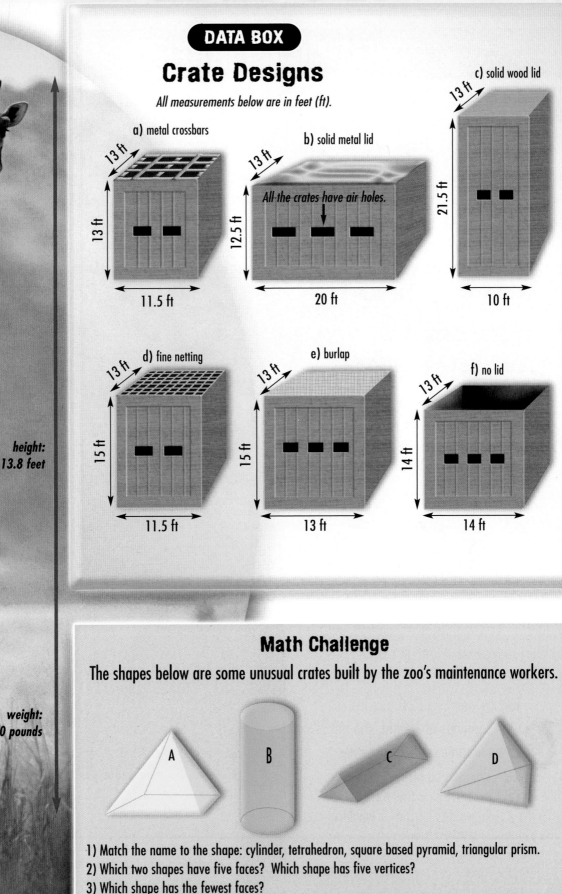

DATA BOX

Crate Designs

All measurements below are in feet (ft).

a) metal crossbars
13 ft
13 ft
11.5 ft

b) solid metal lid
13 ft
12.5 ft
20 ft

All the crates have air holes.

c) solid wood lid
13 ft
21.5 ft
10 ft

d) fine netting
13 ft
15 ft
11.5 ft

e) burlap
13 ft
15 ft
13 ft

f) no lid
13 ft
14 ft
14 ft

height:
13.8 feet

weight:
1,760 pounds

Math Challenge

The shapes below are some unusual crates built by the zoo's maintenance workers.

A   B   C   D

1) Match the name to the shape: cylinder, tetrahedron, square based pyramid, triangular prism.
2) Which two shapes have five faces? Which shape has five vertices?
3) Which shape has the fewest faces?

SEDATING A GIRAFFE

You have arrived at the other zoo and are ready to take Twizzle to your zoo. First, she needs to be sedated, to make her feel calmer and to ensure that she doesn't panic or hurt herself on the journey. To sedate Twizzle, she will be put in her enclosure, and the sedative will be given by injection, using a dart that will be shot from a dart gun. When sedating an animal, it is important that vets take their time and wait for exactly the right moment to shoot the dart. If a vet misses with the first dart, the animal may panic, making it more difficult to get another shot. You need to figure out the correct amount of sedative to give to Twizzle.

Zoo Vet Casebook

To figure out Twizzle's dose of sedative, you have to use decimals and fractions.

1) Show what you know about how decimals and fractions are related by finding the missing numbers in the table below.

?	$1 \div 2$	0.5
?	$1 \div 4$	?
?	?	0.75
$^{1}/_{10}$	?	?

2) What is one-quarter of: 20? 80? 800?

3) What is one-tenth of: 100? 50?

Twizzle weighs 1,760 pounds. For every 2 pounds of weight, she needs 0.25 milligrams (mg) of sedative.

4) How many mg of sedative does Twizzle need?

5) In each milliliter (ml) of injection, there are 50 mg of sedative. How many ml of injection do you need to sedate Twizzle?

Animal Care Fact

When a giraffe is hit by a dart, it sometimes panics and runs, so zoo vets and zookeepers have to make sure the giraffe's enclosure is safe. They check to see that there are no sharp projections sticking out from the walls, and they cover the floor with a deep layer of straw, so it is not slippery.

Animal Care Fact

As Twizzle moves around in her enclosure, the sedative dart will eventually fall out, and her keepers will retrieve it. During the journey to her new home, it is the zoo vet's job to make sure that the giraffe is safe, comfortable, and in the best possible health.

Math Challenge

Test your skill at reading measurement scales.
How much medicine is in each container?

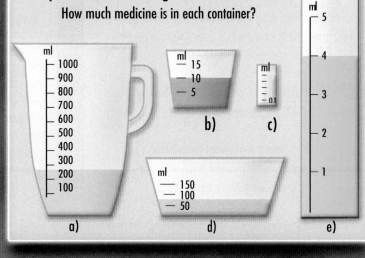

a)

ml
1000
900
800
700
600
500
400
300
200
100

b)

ml
15
10
5

c)

ml
0.1

d)

ml
150
100
50

e)

ml
5
4
3
2
1

TWIZZLE ON THE MOVE!

It takes twenty-four hours for the full effect of the sedative to work on Twizzle, but it will keep her calm for approximately seven days. When Twizzle is fully sedated, she is walked to the traveling crate. A pathway from the door of her enclosure to the back of the crate is lined with burlap to keep her from seeing anything that might frighten or worry her. Twizzle's keepers gently coax her into the crate, tempting her with branches of leaves, which are her favorite food. When Twizzle is safely inside, the crate is gently hoisted onto the truck. Twizzle is ready to go to her new home!

Zoo Vet Casebook

Twizzle must arrive at your zoo as healthy and as calm as possible, so planning the journey carefully is very important.

You have three possible routes to take. To decide on the best route, you need to think about the following:

- The truck will be traveling slowly, so you must choose the shortest route possible.
- The truck had to be very tall to carry Twizzle, so you must avoid low bridges.
- Every three hours, you must stop for thirty minutes to check on Twizzle and give her food and water.
- You must avoid winding roads to make sure Twizzle doesn't fall over.

Look at the three routes in the DATA BOX on page 11. Each square on the routes is ½ hour (30 minutes) of journey time.

1) Which route will give you the fastest journey time?
2) How long will the journey take?

(Don't forget that every three hours you need to add an extra thirty minutes for a checking and feeding stop.)

Animal Care Fact

The driver of the truck must be extremely careful when stopping, accelerating, and turning so the giraffe does not fall over. The driver must also choose quiet places to stop, so the giraffe is not frightened by people or noises while she eats her food and drinks her water.

Giraffe Fact

When giraffes lie down, it takes them a long time to get back on their feet if predators approach, so giraffes usually sleep standing up. Twizzle is safe from predators at the zoo, but her instincts still tell her to sleep standing up.

Giraffe Facts

With their long legs and long necks, giraffes are the tallest animals on Earth, and they can run at speeds of up to 35 miles per hour.

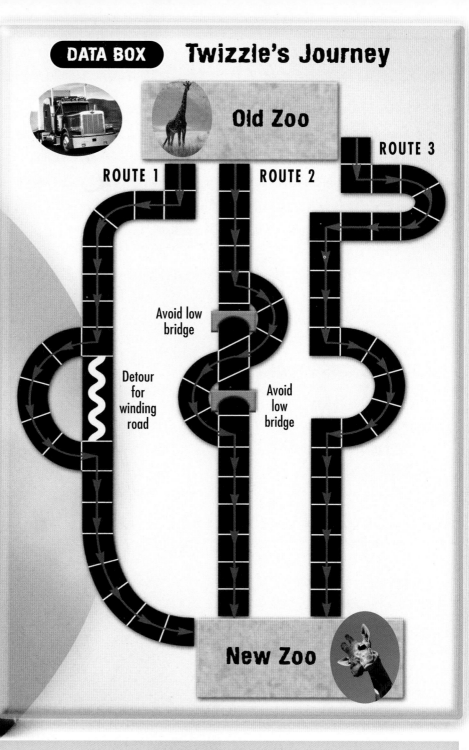

DATA BOX Twizzle's Journey

Old Zoo

ROUTE 1   ROUTE 2   ROUTE 3

Avoid low bridge

Detour for winding road

Avoid low bridge

New Zoo

Math Challenge

Use the routes in the DATA BOX to answer these questions:

1) How many checking and feeding stops would you have to make if you used Route 3?
2) If Twizzle's journey was 30 hours long, how many checking and feeding stops would you have made? (Don't forget that each stop lasts 30 minutes.)
3) If the truck left the old zoo at 9:00 a.m., traveling on Route 2, what time would it be when the truck made Twizzle's second checking and feeding stop?

A NEW HOME FOR TWIZZLE

When she arrives at her new home, Twizzle will need time to recover from her long journey and explore her new surroundings. She will want to find out where the safe areas are in the enclosure and where her food and water comes from. At first, Twizzle is put inside the giraffe enclosure alone. She can see and smell the male giraffe, but she cannot touch him for a few days. The zookeepers quietly keep watch over her and give her lots of browse, vegetables, and fruit, which are foods that contain a large amount of water. It is very important that Twizzle feeds and takes in enough fluids.

Zoo Vet Casebook

A zoo vet has to be able to figure out exactly how much food an animal needs for good health.

In the DATA BOX on page 13, you will see a chart that shows a giraffe's diet divided into hundredths. The chart shows that, as a fraction of the diet, apples are $^{15}/_{100}$, which is 15 parts out of 100, or 15 percent. The symbol % means percent.

1) How much of the giraffe's diet is horse pellets?
2) What percentage is cabbage?
3) How much of the diet is apples and carrots added together?

Animal Care Fact

Animals often will not eat in new surroundings, so powdered glucose (sugar) and electrolytes (salts) are added to their drinking water to give them energy.

Twizzle settles into her new home.

Zoo Vet Diary TWIZZLE MEETS HER MATE

- After a few days, Twizzle and her new mate were allowed to be together for a couple of hours, while the zookeepers kept watch.
- When the zookeepers were satisfied that the two giraffes were getting along, Twizzle was allowed to stay with the male all the time, but only in the house.
- After a few more days, Twizzle and her mate were allowed to be together outside in the enclosure.

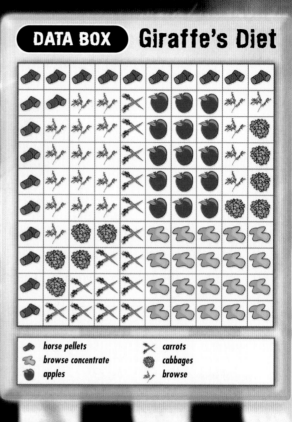

DATA BOX Giraffe's Diet

horse pellets		carrots
browse concentrate		cabbages
apples		browse

Math Challenge

Driving a small electric vehicle called a "gator" around the zoo, Twizzle's keepers have been busy collecting bales of straw to build the giraffe a comfortable bed.

1) The gator is shown partly full of straw bales. How many more bales will fill the gator? Is it 8, 14, 16, or 18?

The straw bales are 6 feet long and 3 feet wide. Twizzle's bed needs to be 24 feet long and 18 feet wide.

2) How many bales are needed to build the bed?
3) If the bed needs to be only half a bale deep, the bales can be sliced in two. How many bales are needed then?

CHECKING FOR PARASITES

I t is spring and time to test all the animals at the zoo for worms. Parasitic worms can harm the animals and cause diarrhea and weight loss. The worms lay their eggs in the animals' stomachs. Then, the eggs are passed out in the animals' feces (solid waste) and lie on the ground. When the animals eat the grass and other plants in their enclosures, they sometimes eat the worm eggs, too. The eggs then go back into the animals' stomachs and develop into more worms. All zoo animals need to be checked twice a year to make sure that parasitic worms don't build up inside them and make them ill.

Zoo Vet Casebook

Wearing gloves, zoo vets and zookeepers collect feces from all the animal enclosures at the zoo. Then they run tests on the feces to check for worms. The numbers of worms in the animals' stomachs depend upon how quickly new worms are born.

If the number of worms doubled every 4 weeks, we could make a table like this one:

WEEKS	0	1	2	3	4	5	6	7	8	9	10	11	12
number of worms, doubling every 4 weeks	1 WORM				2 WORMS				4 WORMS				8 WORMS

Do you understand how the numbers increase? Complete the table below by replacing the question marks with numbers.

WEEKS	0	1	2	3	4	5	6	7	8	9	10	11	12
number of worms, doubling every 3 weeks	1 WORM			2 WORMS			?			?			?
every 2 weeks	1 WORM		2 WORMS		?		?		16 WORMS		?		?
every week	1 WORM	2 WORMS	?	?	?	?	?	?	?	?	?	?	?

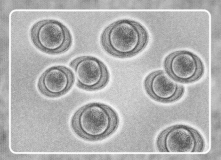

To view Toxocara worm eggs through a microscope, drops of the solution in which the eggs are floating must be placed on a glass slide.

- Some zoo enclosures at the zoo have whole families of animals living there, so a small amount of feces has to be collected from different piles, in the hope that some from each animal will be included.

- Some worms do not lay eggs every day, so feces samples are collected three days in a row.

- Each feces sample is tested in the zoo lab. Water is added to three grams of feces from each sample, and the mixture is shaken up with glass beads, which breaks up the feces.

- The liquid is then sieved into a test tube. The microscopic worm eggs pass through the sieve, with the liquid, into the test tube.

- The test tube is put into a machine called a centrifuge. The centrifuge spins at a very high speed, which forces all of the worm eggs to the bottom of the test tube. The water in the test tube is then poured away.

- A special solution is added to the test tube to make the worm eggs float. Then the eggs can be collected with a pipette and counted under a microscope.

Animal Care Fact

Because zoo animals stay in the same enclosures all the time, they may eat grass or food that contains worm eggs, and the number of eggs in their stomachs can build up quickly. In the wild, animals move from place to place, so there is less chance of their eating worm eggs.

Math Challenge

Toxocara worms are a kind of parasite found in cheetahs.

Female Toxocara worms produce large numbers of eggs.

One Toxocara worm lays 700 eggs in each gram of cheetah feces. If a cheetah has one worm and produces 800 grams of feces in a day, how many eggs will have been laid that day?

WORMING THE PRIMATES

All of the zoo animals are given worming drugs, called anthelmintics, twice a year because, even if the feces samples collected from an enclosure did not show worm eggs, there might still be an animal in that enclosure that has worms. The samples collected might not have included feces from one or more of the animals. An animal that is known to have tested positive for worms is given worming drugs more frequently. Anthelmintic drug powder is added to a small amount of food and given to the animals when they are hungry. So vets will know how much drug the animals have eaten, the rest of their food is given to them after the food with the drug in it is gone.

Zoo Vet Casebook

A zoo vet figures out the correct amount of worming drugs to give each animal by using the animal's body weight. Each of a zoo's primates needs 25 mg of drugs for every pound of its body weight, so the vet needs to know how much each primate weighs.

The DATA BOX on page 17 shows the weights for many of the zoo's primates. Use the information in the DATA BOX to answer the following questions:

1) Which primate is the heaviest?
2) Which primate is the lightest?
3) Name a primate that is heavier than a male lemur but lighter than a female colobus monkey.
4) One of the primates and its traveling crate weigh 6.5 pounds. (When empty, the crate weighs 5.6 pounds.) Which primate is it?

Animal Care Fact

Sometimes, worming drugs are given to animals in the form of a treat by putting them in foods the animals are not normally allowed to eat. Colobus monkeys, spider monkeys, Diana monkeys, and swamp monkeys get their anthelmintic in mashed banana sandwiches. Gorillas and orangutans get theirs in low-sugar, blackcurrant drinks.

Gorilla Fact

One of the gorilla dens at the zoo has a special platform with scales underneath it. A zookeeper puts some of the gorillas' food on the platform and adjusts the scales to show zero. Then the zookeeper lets a gorilla enter the enclosure. When it sits on the platform to eat the food, the gorilla can be weighed.

A zoo vet examines a ring-tailed lemur.

Primate Weight Chart

PRIMATE	ADULT MALE	ADULT FEMALE
gorilla	310 pounds	175 pounds
orangutan	175 pounds	95 pounds
gibbon	15 pounds	15 pounds
ring-tailed lemur	9 pounds	8 pounds
howler monkey	20 pounds	20 pounds
golden lion tamarin	14 ounces	14 ounces
Goeldi monkey	12 ounces	12 ounces
colobus monkey	27 pounds	20 pounds
spider monkey	24 pounds	24 pounds
Diana monkey	21 pounds	21 pounds
swamp monkey	20 pounds	20 pounds

Math Challenge

Try to answer this fun question! On one end of a seesaw are 5 golden lion tamarins and 1 female colobus monkey.

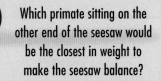

Which primate sitting on the other end of the seesaw would be the closest in weight to make the seesaw balance?

AN EMERGENCY IN WOLF WOODS

You have just received an urgent message. One of the wolves is ill. It has collapsed and is hardly breathing. When you get to Wolf Woods, you see vomit in the enclosure. Wearing gloves, you poke through the vomit to see if you can find a clue that might help you determine why the wolf is ill. The vomit smells very sweet, and you find pieces of foil in it and a substance that looks suspiciously like chocolate. Someone has thrown chocolate candy into the wolves' enclosure. Many animals, including canids (the dog family), can be poisoned by chocolate. All a vet can do is support the animal while it tries to recover.

Zoo Vet Casebook

Zookeepers place the wolf in a large crate and rush it to the treatment room in the zoo hospital. The zoo vet puts a thin tube, called a catheter, into a vein in one of the wolf's front legs. The catheter is used to give emergency drugs and to take blood samples for testing.

You need to give the wolf fluids to maintain its blood pressure and to keep it from going into shock. Every hour, you must give the wolf 5 ml of liquid for every pound it weighs. The wolf weighs 60 pounds.
1) How many milliliters of liquid will you give the wolf each hour?
2) How many milliliters of liquid will the wolf get in 1 minute?
3) How many drops of liquid in one minute? (1 ml = 20 drops)

A wolf bite can be serious. A vet will give a wolf anesthetic gas mixed with oxygen to keep the animal calm during treatments.

Math Challenge

Many animals have special diets and can become very ill or overweight, or can even die, if they eat the wrong foods.

Study the food information in the DATA BOX on page 19.

1) Which animals like to eat: a) grass b) bread c) chicken
2) Which animals must not eat: a) chocolate b) meat
   c) boxwood d) ragwort
3) For which animals might the food bowls below be prepared?

a)   b)   c)

Food Chart

NAME OF ANIMAL	FOODS FOR GOOD HEALTH							POISONOUS FOODS			
	GRASS	CORN	BREAD	CHICKEN	MEAT ON THE BONE	STRAW	VEGETABLES	MEAT	CHOCOLATE	BOXWOOD	RAGWORT
ELEPHANT		✓	✓			✓	✓	✓			
ASIATIC LION				✓	✓				✓		
ZEBRA	✓					✓				✓	
KANGAROO	✓		✓				✓				✓
WOLF				✓	✓				✓		

Zoo Vet Diary SAVING THE WOLF

- When the wolf arrived at the zoo hospital, it was given oxygen, through a mask, to help it breathe and its heart rate and rhythm were checked with a stethoscope. Its temperature, respiration rate (breathing), and blood pressure were monitored at all times. Blood samples were taken, too, and sent straight to the lab for analysis.

- The wolf was given a drug to decrease its fits and to sedate it slightly. Then, it was given fluids.

- After four hours, the wolf started to improve, so it was moved to a recovery pen. During the night, the wolf was checked every three hours to make sure it had not started to have fits again.

- The next day, the wolf was given a small amount of high-energy, easy-to-digest food. Medication was hidden in the food. A week later, the wolf was well enough to go back to Wolf Woods.

Animal Care Fact

Visitors to zoos often throw their own food into the animals' enclosures. Sometimes, they pick leaves from bushes growing outside the enclosure and, without even thinking that they might be poisonous, throw them inside. Notices at zoos asking visitors not to feed the animals should NEVER be ignored.

The zoo vet prepares to treat the wolf.

A PLACE FOR THE RED RIVER HOGS

In a couple of weeks, the zoo will have some more new arrivals. Preparations are under way to welcome three red river hogs that are moving from another zoo. Red river hogs come from Africa and Madagascar. They live in forests and moist savanna woodlands. Red river hogs spend a lot of time rooting in the soil with their noses, looking for food. They can quickly turn a wooded area into a muddy field. The zookeepers have chosen a space for the hogs. It has thick undergrowth and lots of trees. Now you need to help plan the hog's enclosure.

Zoo Vet Casebook

The enclosure will need to be fenced in, and you must remember the following safety precautions:

- The fence around the enclosure must go at least 20 inches under the soil to prevent the hogs from digging it out.
- The fence needs to be at least 5 feet high, to stop visitors from leaning over it.
- To stop visitors from putting their fingers through the main fence and getting bitten, a 3-foot barrier must be built around the edge of the enclosure. The extra barrier should be 3 feet from the main fence.

The enclosure will be a rectangle 300 feet long and 126 feet wide.

1) What is the enclosure's perimeter?
2) If each fencing panel is 12 feet wide, how many panels are needed for the main fence?

Animal Care Fact

When the red river hogs arrive at the zoo, they will go into their new enclosure by walking over a weigh bridge. The zoo vet and zookeepers will then know how much each hog weighs. This information will be useful if the vet ever needs to give the hogs medications or if the females become pregnant.

Hog Fact

Red river hogs are curious, intelligent, and strong. Their senses of smell and hearing are very good, and the hogs communicate with each other constantly, using squeaks, chirrups, and grunts. Red river hogs can weigh up to 265 pounds.

Animal Care Fact

The red river hogs will have a house in their enclosure to give them shelter. Half of the house will have a glass window so that zoo visitors can see the hogs inside. The other half of the house will be closed in to give the hogs some privacy, so they can have an area away from visitors, as well as a quiet place to have babies.

Math Challenge

The zoo wants its animals to have as much space as possible. It also wants visitors to have a good view of the animals, so the longer the fencing, the better.

Look at these drawings of animal enclosures.

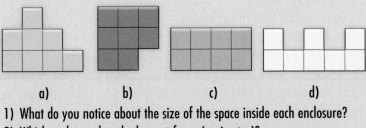

a)   b)   c)   d)

1) What do you notice about the size of the space inside each enclosure?
2) Which enclosure has the longest fence (perimeter)?

AMELIA'S DIET

he red river hogs have settled into their new home, but one of the hogs, named Amelia, is losing weight. There are lots of reasons why Amelia might be getting thinner. She may have mouth pain or a rotten tooth, the zookeepers may not be feeding the hogs enough, or Amelia might have worms. After talking through the problem with the hogs' keepers, you have no clues. When you visit the hogs' enclosure at feeding time, however, you notice that two fatter hogs keep chasing Amelia away from the food. Although Amelia is thin, she does not seem ill and is still bright, alert, and active. You decide to give Amelia her own food and monitor her weight.

Zoo Vet Casebook

Every day at feeding time, you shut Amelia in the hogs' house to eat alone. You also give her extra food. Scales are installed in the house, and on some days, Amelia's food is placed on the scales so you can check her weight while she is eating.

Because Amelia now has enough food, she starts to steadily gain weight.

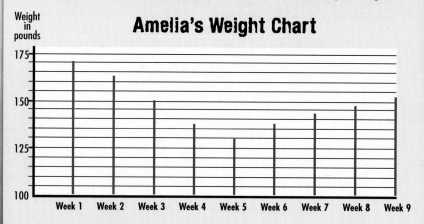

Amelia's Weight Chart

This chart shows changes in Amelia's weight over several weeks. Her healthy weight is shown in Week 1.

1) What is Amelia's healthy weight?
2) How many weeks does Amelia lose weight?
3) How much weight does Amelia gain from week 5 to week 6?
4) In weeks 7, 8, and 9, Amelia gains weight at a steady rate. How do we know this?
5) If Amelia continues to put on weight at this steady rate, how many more weeks will it take for her to nearly reach her healthy weight?

Hog Fact

In the wild, red river hogs feed on a wide range of plants and parts of plants, including grasses, ferns, fungi, roots, leaves, bulbs, and fruits. These hogs also eat insect larvae, frogs, mice, and earthworms. In the zoo, the hogs eat apples, bananas, carrots, cabbage, lettuce, bread, and tomatoes. They are also given vitamins, pellet food, and chicks, for protein.

Animal Care Fact

When the red river hogs first moved into their new home, they were getting a huge amount of food by eating the plants in the enclosure. Now that all of the plants have been eaten, the hogs' food has been increased by about 50 percent. The food is spread around the whole enclosure so each hog has a chance to get more food without being bullied by other hogs. Spreading the food around also gives the hogs more to do during the day.

Math Challenge

The edge of this grid is the fence around the hogs' pen.
Food has been placed at (3,1) and (1,2).
At what other grid points can food be placed away from the fence?

MONEY MATTERS

Many species of wild animals are endangered because humans illegally hunt them or destroy their natural habitats. Many zoos are involved with important conservation and research work. These zoos give endangered animals safe places to live. They also run breeding programs, and they study the animals to find ways to help them in the wild. There are lots of bills to be paid, however, for food, medical care, heat, and wages. Running a zoo costs hundreds of thousands of dollars each year. Zoos raise the funds to pay for their work in lots of ways, including entrance fees, donations, animal adoptions, and gift shop sales.

Zoo Vet Budget

Zoo gift shops sell many fun items to their visitors, and the money the shops make helps pay for the care of the animals.

Use the price list in the DATA BOX on page 25 to help you answer the following money questions.

1) What is the total cost of an orangutan T-shirt and a bean-filled zebra?
2) You pay for a giraffe soft toy with two $1 bills, one quarter, and three dimes. How much change do you get?
3) If you bought a lion hat, how much change would you get from a $10 bill?
4) Postcards are 20 cents each. How many can you buy for $1.60?
5) Which of these can you buy for less than $9?
   a) a pencil case and a set of ballpoint pens
   b) a gorilla and a bean-filled zebra
   c) a notebook and a flamingo soft toy
6) A visitor puts the following coins into a zoo donation box: two quarters, three half dollars, five dimes, four nickels, and eight pennies. How much did this visitor donate altogether?

SAVE THE
ORANGUTANS

Animal Care Fact

Zoo vets make sure that animals living in zoos are kept in the best possible conditions. When animals are happy and healthy, they are more likely to breed. If they breed well, their numbers will increase. Successful breeding sometimes means that endangered animals can be reintroduced in the wild and live in protected areas.

DATA BOX Gift Shop Price List

ballpoint pens (set of three)	$ 3.00
flamingo soft toy (large)	$ 7.99
giraffe soft toy (small)	$ 2.50
orangutan T-shirt	$14.95
lion hat	$ 6.95
notebook	$ 3.75
gorilla soft toy (small)	$ 4.00
pencil case	$ 3.50
postcards (pack of 10)	$ 2.00
zebra (bean-filled)	$ 4.99

This baby orangutan was born in the zoo. With fewer than 25,000 left in the world, orangutans are critically endangered!

Math Challenge

Many zoos run adoption programs, in which you pay a certain amount of money to adopt an animal. You do not get to take the animal home, but your money will help pay for its food and medical care.

The following are some adoption rates:

- $1.50 a year for a llama
- $2.75 a year for an ostrich
- $5.25 a year for an elephant

1) For how long could you adopt a llama or an ostrich if you had $5?
2) If you had $20, which animals could you adopt and for how long?

This baby African elephant was born at the zoo.

27

TWIZZLE HAS A BABY!

Nearly two years have passed since Twizzle arrived at the zoo, and this morning, she gave birth to a calf. You are very worried, however, because, from the moment the calf was born, Twizzle has ignored it. The calf is taking its first unsteady steps, but it hasn't nursed, and Twizzle is starting to become aggressive toward it. You decide that the calf will be taken away from Twizzle for its own safety. Although a mother's milk and colostrum are the best food for a newborn animal, Twizzle is a first time mom, and, sadly, she doesn't seem to know what to do. Hopefully, the next time Twizzle has a baby, she will be a better mother.

Zoo Vet Casebook

Twizzle is taken out of the calving pen, and the zookeepers catch the calf to feed it. For the first few days, the baby will need to be fed colostrum from a bottle, six times a day. After a few days, the colostrum will be replaced with milk.

On day 1, the calf has six regular feedings, starting at 6:00 a.m. and ending at 9:00 p.m.

1) At what times throughout the day is the calf fed?

On day 1, the calf weighs 130 pounds. It is fed one-tenth of its weight.

2) How much is one-tenth of the calf's weight?

3) About how much food is the calf given at each feeding?

4) The calf actually eats only half of the food given at each feeding.
   How much food does the calf eat at each feeding?

5) On day 2, the calf eats three-quarters of the food given at each feeding.
   How much food does the calf eat at each feeding on day 2?

> Twizzle's calf will be bottle-fed until it is fully weaned, at about twelve months old.

Animal Care Fact

Giraffes have a gestation period of 15 to 16 months, which means giraffes are pregnant for 15 to 16 months. Elephants have the longest gestation period of any mammal. They are pregnant for about 22 months — nearly two years!

Bottle-feeding the calf.

Zoo Vet Diary TWIZZLE'S CALF

> Twizzle's calf was over 6 feet tall when it was born!

- We could see that Twizzle was about to give birth because her udders had started to swell and produce milk.
- Twizzle was separated from the male giraffe and video cameras were set up in the enclosure so that we could watch her without disturbing her.
- One morning, Twizzle began pacing up and down and was not interested in her food. Later that day, she gave birth to a male calf.
- Like most giraffes, Twizzle gave birth standing up. When her calf dropped onto the straw on the floor of the enclosure, however, Twizzle just walked away.
- The zookeepers are now rearing Twizzle's baby. After each feeding, they have to make the calf urinate and pass feces by wiping its bottom with a damp cloth. Normally, its mother would do this with her tongue.

DATA BOX Zoo Babies

ANIMAL	GESTATION PERIOD	WEIGHT AT BIRTH
GIRAFFE	15 months	130 pounds
RED RIVER HOG	120 to 127 days	1.5 pounds
PANDA	45 days	3.5 ounces
RING-TAILED LEMUR	134 days	1.75 ounces
ELEPHANT	22 months	200 pounds
GORILLA	8.5 months	4.5 pounds
LION	14 to 15 weeks	3 pounds
MOUSE	21 days	$\frac{1}{25}$ ounce
GIANT ANTEATER	190 days	2.75 pounds
MALAYAN TAPIR	13 months	22 pounds
GRAY WOLF	63 days	1 pound
MOUNTAIN ZEBRA	12 months	55 pounds

Math Challenge
Some of the animals at the zoo become pregnant in March.

The zoo vet needs to know when the animals will have their babies.
1) The timeline below shows which months babies will be born in. Use the DATA BOX above to figure out which animal will be born in which month.

| BABY | BABY | | BABY | BABY | | BABY |
| a | b | | c | d | | e |

MARCH   JUNE   SEPTEMBER   DECEMBER   MARCH

2) Put all the animals in the DATA BOX in order of their birth weight, starting with the heaviest.

MATH TIPS

PAGES 6-7

Zoo Vet Casebook

TOP TIP: You need to ask the following questions about each crate:

- Is the crate tall enough?
- Is it long enough?
- What is the roof made of?

PAGES 8-9

Metric Measurements

Doses of medicines and drugs are typically measured in milligrams and milliliters, which are part of the metric system of weights and measures. Below you will see the relationships of some common metric measurements.

Weight
1 milligram (mg)
1 gram (g) = 1,000 mg
1 kilogram (kg) = 1,000 g
1 tonne = 1,000 kg

Volume
1 milliliter (ml)
1 centiliter (cl) = 10 ml
1 deciliter (dl) = 100 ml
1 liter (l) = 1,000 ml

Length
1 millimeter (mm)
1 centimeter (cm) = 10 mm

1 meter (m) = 100 cm
1 kilometer (km) = 1,000 m

PAGES 12-13

Zoo Vet Casebook

Percent is a special form of a fraction. It means "part of 100." For example: 50% is $^{50}/_{100}$, 25% is $^{25}/_{100}$.

Percentages are very useful for comparing amounts. They are often used in stores to show how much prices are lowered for a sale.

If something was for sale for $10.00 you might see
50% OFF (which would make the price $5.00)
25% OFF (which would make the price $7.50)
75% OFF (which would make the price $2.50)

PAGES 14-15

Math Challenge

When multiplying hundreds, such as 200 x 300, you can multiply 2 x 3, which is 6, then add zeros to make 60,000. Look at the total number of zeros in 200 and 300 to know how many zeros to add.

For example:
- 2 x 300 = 600
- 20 x 300 = 6,000
- 200 x 300 = 60,000

PAGES 16-17

TOP TIP: Converting measurements given in different units to the same unit can make comparisons and calculations easier.

Example: 15 pounds and 12 ounces can be compared as either 240 ounces and 12 ounces or as 15 pounds and 0.75 pounds. (Remember: 1 pound = 16 ounces.)

PAGES 20-21

Zoo Vet Casebook

TOP TIP: Perimeter is the distance all the way around a shape. You can figure out the perimeter of a rectangle in three different ways:
- Add all four sides.
- Add one long and one short side, then double the answer.
- Double the length of the long side, then double the length of the short side and add the totals together.

Math Challenge

TOP TIP: To find the perimeter, you can count the outside edges of the squares. The space inside the perimeter is called the "area."

Zoo Vet Casebook

This type of chart is known as a bar graph. In this graph, you could connect the tops of the bars to make a continuous line graph. The numbers along the left-hand side do not start at 0 pounds because: 1) hogs will not ever weigh 0 pounds, and 2) starting at 100 pounds makes the graph clearer.

Math Challenge

When you use a grid, you read along the bottom of the grid first, then up the side.

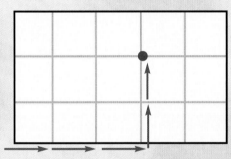

Example: a grid reference of **(3,2)** means **3 steps** along the bottom, then **2 steps** up to find the exact spot.

Zoo Vet Budget

Remember that, when you are shopping, to figure out total costs, you can round up prices to approximate amounts. You can round $3.99 up to $4 to make figuring in your head easier, but don't forget to take 1 cent off the total at the end to get the exact amount.

Rounding up can also help you calculate how much change you will receive.

Example: The lion hat costs $3.95. If you pay with a $10 bill, you can round up $3.95 to four dollars, and four dollars from ten dollars leaves six dollars. Your change, then, will be six dollars and five cents.

Math Challenge

A timeline is a kind of number line. Number lines are continuous and reach forever in both directions. Number lines can help us better understand some of the number problems we are trying to figure out.

March   April   May

This number line is a timeline.

March
1   2   3   4   5

This number line is also a timeline.

March 1

12 noon 1:00p.m. 2:00p.m. 3:00p.m. 4:00p.m.

This number line is another timeline.

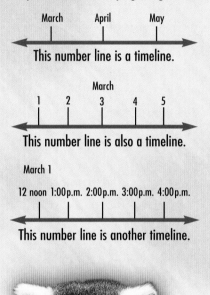

ANSWERS

Zoo Vet Casebook

1) e 2) Crate "e" is the best choice because it is taller than Twizzle and big enough for her to turn around in, and it has a burlap roof. 3) 1.2 feet

Math Challenge

1) The names of the shapes are:

A – square based pyramid

B – cylinder

C – triangular prism

D – tetrahedron

2) Shapes A and C each have five faces. Shape A has five vertices.
3) Shape B has the fewest faces. One curved face (along its length) and two circular faces (one at each end).

PAGES 8-9

Zoo Vet Casebook

1) The completed table should look like this:

½	1 ÷ 2	0.5
¼	1 ÷ 4	0.25
¾	3 ÷ 4	0.75
¹⁄₁₀	1 ÷ 10	0.1

2) One quarter of: 20 is 5, 80 is 20, 800 is 200.
3) One tenth of: 100 is 10, 50 is 5.
4) Twizzle needs 220 mg of sedative.
5) You need 4.4 ml of injection to sedate Twizzle.

PAGES 8-9 continued

Math Challenge

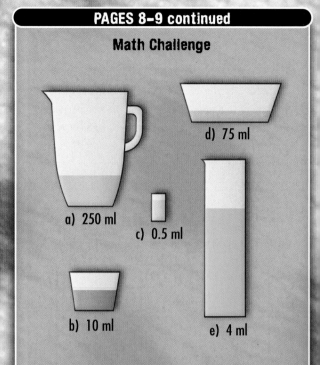

a) 250 ml

c) 0.5 ml

b) 10 ml

d) 75 ml

e) 4 ml

PAGES 10-11

Zoo Vet Casebook

1) Route 2 will give you the fastest journey time.
2) On Route 2, the journey will take 11 hours.

Math Challenge

1) You would make 4 stops.
2) You would have made 8 stops.
3) The second stop would be at 3:30 p.m.

PAGES 12-13

Zoo Vet Casebook

1) ⅕ (²⁰⁄₁₀₀), or 20%, of the diet is horse pellets.
2) 10%, or ¹⁄₁₀, of the diet is cabbage.
3) Apples and carrots together are 30% (³⁄₁₀) of the diet.

Math Challenge

1) 14 more bales will fill the gator.
2) 24 bales are needed to build Twizzle's bed.
3) 12 bales are needed if the bales are sliced in two.

Zoo Vet Casebook

1) The enclosure's perimeter is 852 feet.
2) 71 fencing panels are needed.

Math Challenge

1) The amount of space inside all enclosures is the same.
2) Enclosure "d" has the longest fence (perimeter).

Zoo Vet Casebook

1) 170 pounds 2) 4 weeks 3) 7 pounds
4) Because the bars go up by the same amount
(5 pounds) each week.   5) 3 weeks

Math Challenge

Food can be placed at points (1,1), (2,1), (2,2),and (3,2)

Zoo Vet Casebook

The completed table should look like this:

WEEKS	0	1	2	3	4	5	6	7	8	9	10	11	12
number of worms, doubling every 3 weeks	1 WORM			2 WORMS			4			8			16
every 2 weeks	1 WORM		2 WORMS		4		8		16		32		64
every week	1 WORM	2 WORMS	4	8	16	32	64	128	256	512	1,024	2,048	4,096

Math Challenge

The toxocara worm will have laid 560,000 eggs that day.

Zoo Vet Casebook

1) The male gorilla is the heaviest.
2) The Goeldi monkeys are the lightest.
3) A male or female gibbon is heavier than a male lemur but lighter than a female colobus monkey.
4) a golden lion tamarin.

Math Challenge

A spider monkey has the closest weight to balance the seesaw.

Zoo Vet Budgets

1) $19.94 2) 5 cents 3) $3.05 4) 8 postcards
5) a) a pencil case and a set of ballpoint pens ($6.50) and
   b) a gorilla and a bean-filled zebra ($8.99) 6) $2.78

Math Challenge

1) You could adopt a llama for 3 years or an ostrich for
1 year. (You could also adopt a llama and an ostrich
   for 1 year.)
2) With $20, you could adopt a llama for 13 years,
an ostrich for 7 years, or an elephant for 3 years.
(You could also adopt all three animals for 2 years.)

Zoo Vet Casebook

1) 300 ml   2) 5 ml   3) 100 drops

Math Challenge

1) a) grass: zebra and kangaroo
   b) bread: elephant and kangaroo
   c) chicken: Asiatic lion and wolf
2) a) chocolate: Asiatic lion and wolf
   b) meat: elephant
   c) boxwood: zebra
   d) ragwort: kangaroo
3) a) Asiatic lion and wolf
   b) elephant and kangaroo
   c) elephant and zebra

Zoo Vet Casebook

1) The calf is fed at 6:00 a.m., 9:00 a.m., 12:00 noon,
3:00 p.m., 6:00 p.m., and 9:00 p.m.
2) 13 pounds 3) 2 pounds 4) 1 pound 5) $1\frac{1}{2}$ pounds

Math Challenge

1) a) gray wolf (May) b) lion (June)
c) giant anteater (September) d) gorilla (November)
e) mountain zebra (March)

2) elephant, giraffe, mountain zebra, Malayan tapir,
gorilla, lion, giant anteater, red river hog, gray wolf,
panda, ring-tailed lemur, mouse

GLOSSARY

ANESTHETIC a drug or a gas used to put an animal to sleep, so it will not, for example, feel pain during an operation

BREED to produce offspring by joining male and female reproductive cells

BREEDING PROGRAMS organized efforts to match up animals, especially endangered animals, for breeding, helping to build a large and healthy population of that type of animal to ensure that its species does not die out

BROWSE tender leaves and twigs of trees and shrubs, which is the type of food that certain animals would eat in the wild

CATHETER a thin, flexible plastic tube that can be inserted into the body for giving medicines or drugs or for drawing out liquids, such as blood or urine

CENTRIFUGE a machine that spins or whirls rapidly, using centrifugal force, which moves objects or parts of objects outward from the center of rotation, to separate the components of substances or to remove moisture from a substance

COLOSTRUM the first milk produced by a mother to feed her baby, which is particularly high in protein and contains antibodies to help kill germs and viruses

ENDANGERED having a population that is growing smaller, due to hunting or loss of habitat, and is in danger of dying out, or becoming extinct

FECES the solid bodily waste that is passed by an animal through its anus

GESTATION PERIOD the length of time that an animal needs to develop in its mother's body before being born

INSTINCTS behaviors, or ways of acting in specific situations, which are natural to an animal, not taught but, rather, inherited from its ancestors and characteristic of its species

LARVAE the wingless, wormlike forms of newly hatched insects

PARASITIC describing an organism that needs to live in, or on, the body of another organism to survive, using the host organism to get essential nutrients

PIPETTE a very small and very thin glass or plastic rod

PRIMATES the animal group that includes humans and other animals, such as monkeys and apes, that are similar to humans in many ways

SAVANNA areas of land, with mainly grasses and brush for vegetation, that are normally located in warm climates and have distinct dry and rainy seasons

SEDATED calmed down as a result of being given an injection of a drug or some other substance that produces a quieting effect or sleepiness

STETHOSCOPE an instrument used by doctors, veterinarians, and other medical professionals to listen to sounds produced inside the body, especially by the heart and lungs

VERTICES the points or angles at which two surfaces meet or intersect

WEANED no longer drinking only mother's milk or a substitute liquid as a main source of food, or nutrients

Measurement Conversions

1 inch = 2.54 centimeters (cm)
1 foot = 0.3048 meters (m)
1 mile = 1.609 kilometers (km)
1 pound = 0.4536 kilograms (kg)
1 ounce = 28.33 grams (g)